He
Made
You
Beautiful

Devotions and Prayers for a deeper
relationship with God

Phyllis Sosa Lourenço

WESTBOW·
PRESS
A DIVISION OF THOMAS NELSON
& ZONDERVAN

WestBow Press books may be ordered through booksellers or by contacting:

WestBow Press
A Division of Thomas Nelson & Zondervan
1663 Liberty Drive
Bloomington, IN 47403
www.westbowpress.com
1 (866) 928-1240

ISBN: 978-1-4908-6517-1 (sc)
ISBN: 978-1-4908-6516-4 (e)

Printed in the United States of America.

WestBow Press rev. date: 01/06/2015

CONTENTS

CHAPTER 1

Love

"For the entire law is fulfilled in keeping this one command: "Love your neighbor as you love yourself." Galatians 5:14

Our ability to love others comes from God. We can only give and show love when we have God in our hearts. If you want to learn how to love other people, you have to first understand and feel how much God loves you. When you feel that unconditional love you're not going to be as angry as you've been in the past with people. Maybe you've been hurt in your past. Mentally, physically and emotionally. If you're filled with anger and bitterness, you're not going to be able to love anybody else. You have to let God heal your heart so his love can flow through you. It is impossible to love others until you learn to love yourself first.

Lord, help me to love like you. Fill my heart with a desire to love. Satisfy me and help me to speak and walk in love. Lord, thank you for loving me with a love that will never run out. I want to experience your love in a deeper way than I have ever experienced before. Let your loves grow in me like a flower, beautiful and acceptable in your eyes. I love you Lord with all of my heart. In Jesus name, Amen.

NOTES

_____

CHAPTER 2

The Peace of God

"Peace I leave to you; my peace I give to you. I do not give to you as the world gives. Do not let your hearts be troubled and do not be afraid." John 14:27

Do you need peace in your life? Peace comes from when you fix your eyes on God and meditate in his presence. Peace comes by putting your confidence in him and believing that he will stand right beside you through your most difficult and stressful times. If you genuinely believe in his word and what it says, it will guide you and you will find yourself centered in his peace.

When you receive his peace you can endure anything that comes your way because your focus is on him.

Lord, I need more of you in my life. I need more of your peace. There are many things in my life that I can't control or fix. Sometimes I'm really stressed. Sometimes I'm really down. Sometimes I cry. Lord, remove anything in my life that's causing me stress, grief, and sorrow. Be with me and protect me. Give me complete peace today. In Jesus name, Amen.

NOTES

_____

CHAPTER 3

Forgiveness

"And when you stand praying, if you hold anything against anyone, forgive them, so that your Father in heaven may forgive your sins." Mark 11:25

Refusing to forgive others is a sin. If you receive forgiveness for your sins, then you must give it to others. God wants you to be at peace and for that to occur, you must replace anger and bitterness with forgiveness. Forgiving others is sometimes very difficult. He understands your hurt, but if you don't forgive others, you won't break free. If you're having difficulty forgiving, take a moment to examine your reasons. Remember that forgiveness is about you, not about them. The pain and anguish will not subside until you make the choice to forgive them.

Lord, I'm sorry for all the times I've been unloving, angry, and disrespectful. Teach me the right way to forgive. Cleanse me of all bitterness and resentment and give me a heart like yours to forgive. In Jesus name, Amen.

NOTES

_____

CHAPTER 4

Patience

"But those who hope in the Lord will renew their strength. They will soar on the wings like eagles; they will run and not grow weary; they will walk and not be faint." Isaiah 40:31

Why is being patient so difficult at times? Why does God make us wait? What type of situations test our patience? Everyone struggles with patience. God uses trials, difficulties, and people in our lives to develop patience in us. God is always patient with us so why are we not with him? We forget that God has good reasons for making us wait. If we can't wait for the small things, how can we wait for something bigger? Remember that complaining is the opposite of patience. Complaining puts all the focus on you instead of on him.

Lord, it's so hard to wait. To wait for you to answer my prayers. To wait for you to move in my life. Deepen my trust in you Lord when my flesh is weak. I cannot be strong on my own. I know that you have great plans for me. I just have a hard time waiting. Please fill my heart with patience. Help me to not complain and to trust more in you. In Jesus name, Amen.

NOTES

CHAPTER 5

Thankfulness

"Give thanks to the Lord, for he is good.
His love endures forever." Psalm 136:1

Everything you have is a gift from God. There are three reasons why you should thank God. The first reason is because of who he is. The second reason is because he is your daily provider. And the third reason is because he loves you so much that he gave his only son to die for your sins. God is everything you ask him to be. He is your friend, your shelter and a comforter. Thank him for your friends, for your faith and for your family. Thank him for the food you have on your table and your wellness. Show him that you are grateful. The more you thank him, the more you will experience his goodness.

Lord, thank you for being who you are in my life. Thank you for giving me another day to be in your presence. Thank you for your blessings and promises. Thank you for being with me when I need you. Thank you for giving me joy in times of sorrow. Thank you for my family and friends. Thank you for my job and my education. Thank you for love and peace. Lord I give you my heart, my soul and mind. I treasure your word. In Jesus name, Amen.

NOTES

CHAPTER 6

Faith

"Now faith is being sure of what we hope for and certain of what we do not see." Hebrews 11:1

Faith is enabled when you act. Without faith it is impossible to please God (Hebrews 11:6). You grow in faith by hearing and studying the word of God. When you doubt God you lack in faith. When you ask, you must believe that what you're asking for, you will receive. When Jesus said peace be still in the storm, the disciples witnessed a miracle, but they were consumed with fear. Jesus was with them and they waited until the last minute to ask for help. It's the same in your life, don't wait until the situation is hard to manage. Ask for help and put your faith into action!

Lord, I trust in you. I trust in your ways. Be my rock and my protection. Set me free from fear and continue to work in my life. Open my eyes to see you. Open my ears to hear you. Lord your word says that faith comes by hearing the word of God. So today I will trust in your word. Today I will put my faith into action. In Jesus name, Amen.

NOTES

_____

CHAPTER 7

Friendship

"Oil and perfume make the heart glad, and the sweetness of a friend comes from his earnest counsel." Proverbs 27:9

How can we recognize true friendships? Signs include a mutual desire for a true relationship and a common bond of some sort. True friendships involve caring and desiring to see one another grow and develop in all aspects of life. Friendship isn't something that takes place overnight. Friendship takes time and commitment. Time to build, share memories, and time to invest in each other's growth. Real friends encourage one another and forgive. Real friends support during tough times and struggles. If you don't have true friendships, then ask God for some.

Lord, give me true friends in my life. If there are any relationships that I'm involved in that doesn't please you, separate me from them. I want to true friends who will build me up and encourage me. In Jesus name, Amen.

NOTES

CHAPTER 8

Obedience

"Love the Lord your God and keep his requirements, his decrees, his laws and his commands always." Deuteronomy 11:1

When we obey God, we can trust that he will show his goodness and love for us. If we fail to believe his word, we will find it difficult to obey him. Why is obedience so important to him? The simplest reason is because it's our obligation. Obedience should come from your heart. We should obey his commandments because we want to please him. We must submit ourselves entirely to him. Obeying him is a fundamental part in our walk with him. If there are any areas in your life where you know you're not being obedient in, work on it today.

Lord, you have called me to be obedient. I am not perfect, but I desire to please you. Help me to be obedient to your commandments. Help me to understand them. Give me the desire to obey you with all of my heart. In Jesus name, Amen.

NOTES

CHAPTER 9

Purity and Holiness

*"Create in me a clean heart,
O God, and renew a steadfast
spirit within me." Psalm 51:10*

We have to grow in purity and in holiness. Have you had these thoughts before? God just doesn't understand me, he simply doesn't want me to have fun anymore, God is just going to make my life miserable. These thoughts are lies. He created you and so he knows every detail in your life. He understands the best way to live life because he created life. To be holy and pure, you have to see purity and holiness from God's perspective. Trust in God to clean your heart because he is capable of doing it if you allow him.

Lord, give me a clean heart. Wash away all the impurities. Help me to live a lifestyle of holiness. Lord in everything I do, let it be holy and acceptable in your eyes. I am your servant lord. In Jesus name, Amen.

NOTES

CHAPTER 10

Wisdom

*"If any of you lacks wisdom, you
should ask God, who gives generously
to all without finding fault, and it
will be given to you."* James 1:5

Need wisdom? God's wisdom is unlimited
so don't be embarrassed to ask. Without
wisdom how can you make good decisions
and choices? When you ask it is important
to ask faithful and without doubting (James
1:67). There are two different types of
wisdom. Worldly wisdom and Godly wisdom.
Worldly wisdom is the use of knowledge and
information on human understanding. Godly

wisdom is the ability to see things from God's perspective. We need his wisdom, each and every day in our lives. We are faced with many different situations that require us to have wisdom to show us what to do. He yearns for us to have his wisdom because he doesn't want us to struggle with everything in our lives.

Lord, I lack in wisdom. I need your wisdom to help me make the right choices and decisions. Instruct me and teach me in the way I should go. Direct my steps Lord. Give me a heart that is willing to obey you. In Jesus name, Amen.

NOTES

_____

CHAPTER 11

Trials and Tribulations

"I have told you these things to you, so that in me you may have peace. In this world you will have trouble. But take heart! I have overcome the world." John 16:33

Following God isn't easy. We are persecuted and ridiculed for our faith. Why does God allow us to go through trials and tribulations? Well following God doesn't make us immune to life's trials and tribulations. It's not an easy button. We ask ourselves, why would a good loving God allow these things such as the death of a family member, sickness, financial struggles, fear and worry? Well, we know that his word teaches us that he works all things for good (Romans 8:28). So that means everything we go through he is with us. Every struggle comes with a purpose and a reward. Don't give up. Be encouraged because God will never leave you alone.

Lord, I know that every struggle I face you are with me. God when I am weak you are with me. God when I feel like giving up, you are with me. Lord, when my flesh is weak, give me strength. Lord, when my enemies want to see me fall, give me victory. Lord, keep my eyes fixed on you. In Jesus name, Amen.

NOTES

CHAPTER 12

The Holy Spirit

"But the advocate, the Holy Spirit, whom the Father will send in my name, will teach you all things and will remind you of everything I have said to you." John 14:26

As you grow spiritually, the Holy Spirit needs to have more control in the areas of your life. The Holy Spirit is gentle and comforts us when we are hurting. The Holy Spirit helps us to stop sinning and do the things that please God. As you rely more on the Holy Spirit, sin becomes more apparent in your life. Open up yourself to the Holy Spirit and allow him to come into your heart.

Lord, I invite your Holy Spirit in my life. Come now and kindle a fire in my heart. Help me not live according to my old ways. I want to feel you in my life. I want to know more of you. In Jesus name, Amen.

NOTES

CHAPTER 13

Living Righteously

"I put on righteousness as my clothing; justice was my robe and my turban." Job 29:14

Living righteously is something we simply cannot do without God in our lives. Righteousness means the character of being right or just. Our desires must come from the heart to follow God. He declared us to be righteous. One of the first things we should do in order to live righteously is, learning how to be humble to accept that God's word is right. Then, confess our sins by repentance, and follow his commandments. It is important to accept discipline and correction. Change doesn't happen overnight, but when we fight off temptations and sinful desires, he will in turn help us to live righteously. So are you living righteously for God?

Lord, help me to accept discipline and correction. I know that you love me and I know that you want the best for me. In Jesus name, Amen.

NOTES

CHAPTER 14

Total Surrender

*Then he said to them all: "Whoever
wants to be my disciple must deny
themselves and take up their cross
daily and follow me." Luke 9:23*

We need to let go and let God work.
Sometimes we put too much focus on how
we can fix something instead of letting
God handle it. The Bible tells us to cast
our fears to him (Psalm 55:22). Sometimes
we are not even sure of what to let go of.
Sometimes we might be holding tightly
to something we think is good. When

you surrender to God, you must give everything to him. Every part of yourself. That means your struggles, worries, and pain. When you surrender completely, you are trusting in his purpose and his plan. When you surrender to God you will rely more on him instead of trying to control the situation.

Lord, I surrender today. I give you all of my worries and struggles. I give you my pain and my tears. Come into the secret places of my heart. I surrender all to you: my health, my relationships, my family, my successes and failures. I release it, and let it go. I surrender to you the promises I have kept and the promises I have failed to keep.

I surrender my weaknesses and strengths to you. I surrender my emotions, my fears and my insecurities. I surrender my entire life to you. In Jesus name, Amen.

NOTES

_____

CHAPTER 15

Gifts from God

"Every of you should use whatever gift you have received to serve others, as faithful stewards of God's grace in its various forms." 1 Peter 4:10

God has given you amazing gifts. When he gives you a gift he expects you to use it. It's like a flower, if you nurture it, it will grow. If you don't, it will die. If you have a gift from God and you're afraid to use it or if you get lazy and don't use it to serve others, God will give it to someone else. When you use your gift, you bless those around you. Even if your life is busy, God will give you a way to be able to use your gift. When you put your gifts to use, according to his purpose, great things happen. Whether you're a musician or a painter, a dancer or a teacher, he gave you those abilities to serve others.

Lord, thank you for the gifts I have. Help me to manifest and practice my gifts. Lord, I want to please you and minister to others. Let my gifts encourage others to use their gifts. In Jesus name, Amen.

NOTES

_____

CHAPTER 16

Heart of Worship

"God is spirit, and his worshipers must worship in the spirit and truth." John 4:24

What makes worship so important? The purpose of our worship is to glorify, praise, exalt, and honor God. Worship is like intimacy, it's between you and him. Our worship must show our adoration and loyalty to him. He wants worship not only on our lips, but also in our hearts. So it must be sincere. When was the last time you went before God, and just listened? We know that worship can be expressed with singing and church services, but there comes a point where our worship must include being still before his presence. Sometimes God calls us to be still to recognize and understand that he is God, our creator. Set aside a day to spend time with him.

Lord, teach me to come before you with reverence in my heart. At this moment, I want to express how much I love you Lord. Help me to understand the true meaning of worship and to learn to worship you in spirit and in truth. In Jesus name, Amen.

NOTES

CHAPTER 17

When God says "No"

"For I know the plans I have for you,"
declares the Lord, "plans to prosper
you and not to harm you, plans to
give you hope and a future.

God does answer all prayers. Have you ever prayed to God and had him answer you by saying "No?" It's frustrating isn't it? Sometimes you don't even know how to deal with that answer. Let's be honest, sometimes we pray for the wrong things. Sometimes we pray for things that could harm our relationship with God. Sometimes we ask for things that would be harmful to us spiritually. These "good" things could possibly cause us to lose sight of him. As hard as it is to admit, we don't see the bigger picture. God always knows what's best for us. He has something better in mind.

Lord, there are many times I prayed for certain things. I've cried many times wondering if you're hearing me. Sometimes I felt so weak and unable to go on. But Lord, thank you for being with me. Even through the pain and anger, you were always there. Forgive me for acting in anger because I couldn't get what I wanted. I'm sorry Lord. Help me to trust more in you. Help me to realize that you have everything in control. In Jesus name, Amen.

NOTES

CHAPTER 18

Dreams and Visions

"And afterward, I will pour out my Spirit on all people. Your sons and daughters will prophesy, your old men will dream dreams, your young men will see visions." Joel 2:28

God speaks to us in dreams and visions. How do we know if a dream or vision is from God? No dream or vision that goes directly against what is written in his word is from God. We must ask God for the spirit of discernment to know right from wrong. Sometimes we describe discernment as a gut feeling. If you have a hard time remembering dreams and visions, write them down as soon as you wake up, so that you can pray about them.

Lord, some of my dreams and visions don't make sense. Lord, give me a spirit of discernment. Help me to be aware of my surroundings in my dreams. I trust that what you're revealing to me has a purpose and plan. In Jesus name, Amen.

NOTES

_____

CHAPTER 19

Testimony

"I proclaim your saving acts in the great assembly; I do not seal my lips, Lord, as you know. I do not hide your righteousness in my heart; I speak of your faithfulness and your saving help. I do not conceal your love and your faithfulness from the great assembly." Psalm 40:9-10

There is power in your testimony. Your testimony is about what you have experienced. By sharing your testimony, you create a connection with others who share your path, or who are on the path now. It makes people feel they are not alone.

Which gives them hope. Remember the story of the blind man in John 9? Jesus healed the man in two stages. Because of his faith he was healed. The glory of God was seen in him. Don't be ashamed of your testimony. No matter how little or big your testimony may be, you can change a life!

Lord, I want to testify of all the great things you have done for me. Without you I wouldn't be here. Thank you for giving me strength to overcome my struggles. I pray that my testimony would be a blessing to others. In Jesus name, Amen.

NOTES

CHAPTER 20

Judging others

"Brothers and sisters do not slander one another. Anyone who speaks against a brother or sister or judges them speaks against the law and judges it. When you judge the law, you are not keeping it, but sitting in judgment on it. Therefore is only one lawgiver and judge, the one who is able to save and destroy. But you-who are you to judge your neighbor?" James 4:11-12

It's pretty easy to fall into the habit of judging others. Sometimes we judge people based on their appearance. Like a homeless man, on the street begging for money. We tend to wonder how he got there and if he's a drug addict or an alcoholic. When in reality, he could just have a hard life. We judge a stranger because of the way they are dressed, when in reality, maybe that's all they could afford. It is God's job to judge not us. Instead of judging others, embrace them with kindness and love them. Talk to them, see what they could be going through, because God might want to show you something through them.

Lord, I admit that I have judged others based on their appearance and the way they talked. I didn't give them a chance. I'm sorry for treating them wrong. Help me to be more kind and loving. Lord, even when I see a homeless person, help me to have the heart to give. In Jesus name, Amen.

NOTES

CHAPTER 21

Keeping the Sabbath Day Holy

"Remember the Sabbath day by keeping it holy." Exodus 20:8

All seven days of the week belong to God. The seventh day has a special significance, because God completed creation in six days, and rested on the seventh day. He made this particular day holy to him, commanding his people to rest. God is very passionate about the Sabbath and he wants us to be as well. But what does it mean to keep the Sabbath holy? It means to set it apart from any other day and devote yourself completely to God.

Lord, help me to keep the Sabbath day holy. Lord, I want to rest in your presence and deepen my relationship with you. Remove any distractions that are blocking me from having this day with you. In Jesus name, Amen.

Notes

_____

CHAPTER 22

Giving Back to God

"Give and it will be given to you. A good measure, pressed down, shaken together and running over, will be poured into your lap. For with the measure you use, it will be measured to you." Luke 6:38

The story of Hannah (1 Samuel 1:1-28) is a remarkable story about new life and deliverance. Elkanah had two wives, Peninnah who had children and Hannah who had none. Hannah was very miserable. On top of all that, because Peninnah was so jealous that Elkanah loved Hannah more than her, she provoked and tormented

Hannah. Eventually Hannah couldn't stand it anymore and she decided to do something about her situation. Instead of staying in her despair, she decided to pray to God for a son. She made a promise that she would give the child back to God. As she was pouring out her heart to God in anguish at the Tabernacle, the priest, Eli, thought she was drunk and rebuked her. But then he heard her explanation and asked the Lord to grant her request. God then granted her a son and she named him Samuel. Hannah kept her son until he was weaned and gave him to Eli. She was obedient to her promise and her heart rejoiced. What can you learn from this story? Giving back to God is important. When you give, he will bless you for your obedience.

Lord, I want to be faithful to the promises I've made, big and small. Lord, hear my desperate cries. Deliver me from pain. Restore the sorrow with joy. In Jesus name, Amen.

NOTES

_____

CHAPTER 23

Fasting

"So I turned to the Lord God and pleaded with him in prayer and petition, in fasting, and in sackcloth and ashes." Daniel 9:3

Fasting is abstaining from all food and taking in nothing but water. The reason why we should fast is to strengthen prayer, seek his guidance, and seek deliverance and protection. Fasting is an important part of having a healthy relationship with God. When you fast you can pray for specific needs for yourself or others. You can also fast from time spent on the phone, or watching TV, or playing games. When you begin fasting, you will see the changes in your walk with God. The presence of God will become closer and clearer to you.

Lord, touch me deeply today. I want to know you. Turn my eyes away from the things of the world. Let me see you Lord, connect me to you. Transform me, cleanse me, and purify me. In Jesus name, Amen.

NOTES

_____

CHAPTER 24

God's Temple

"Do you not know that your bodies are temples of the Holy Spirit, who is in you, whom you have received from God? You are not your own; you were bought at a price. Therefore honor God with your bodies." 1 Corinthians 6:19-20

Your body is a gift from God. He created your body as a place to dwell in. Wherever you are, wherever you go, you take him with you. You cannot expect your body to be a holy place for God to dwell in, if sin is present. It is your responsibility to keep your body holy. What you do with your body matters when you are following God. Your body needs to be treated with respect and care. Every part of your body is intended for the glorification of God. So ask yourself today, am I honoring God with my body? Is God dwelling inside of me?

Lord, I've failed to honor you with my body. I've used my body for my own desires. Forgive me of my sins. Help me to glorify you with my body in everything that I do. Lord, I want my body to be a place for you to dwell in. In Jesus name, Amen.

NOTES

CHAPTER 25

The Power of the Tongue

"The tongue has the power of life and death, and those who love it will eat its fruits." Proverbs 18:21

What we speak with our mouths can have a big impact on our own lives, as well as the lives of others. In other words, you can manifest God's blessings by speaking life into your situation or you can call in those things that you really don't want to happen by speaking negatively. Your life is determined by the words you speak. You have the power to choose life or death. If you are going around constantly saying negative words then you are going to reap the results of your words. If you wake up in the morning saying this is going to be a horrible and miserable day, then you can bet it will be. Today start your day with some positive declarations and you will immediately see the changes.

Lord, I speak life into every situation that I'm going through. Thank you for new blessings and new beginnings. Thank you for your presence in my home, in my family and in my relationships. I will be successful. I will not be defeated. I will overcome every struggle and every pain. In Jesus name, Amen.

NOTES

CHAPTER 26

Worship of False Gods

"You shall have no other gods before me. You shall not make for yourself an image in the form of anything in heaven above or on earth beneath or in the waters below. You shall not bow down to them or worship them; for I, the Lord your God, am a jealous God, punishing children for the sin of the parents to the third and fourth generation of those who hate me, but showing love to a thousand generations of those who love me and keep my commandments." Exodus 20: 3-6

The root of idolatry is rebelliousness. Anything we use in order to meet our physical, emotional or spiritual needs, apart from God himself, is an idol. When we put our full attention on these idols, we push God out and leave no room for him. God hates anything that causes us to be unfaithful to him. He wants you to put him first in your life. In your thoughts and in your prayers. He loves you and will not put up with anything that steals your love away from him. Who are you putting first in your life?

Lord, I come before you realizing that I have placed some things in my life that I have created as an idol. Forgive me for not putting you first in my life. Kindle a desire in me to love you and only you. In Jesus name, Amen.

NOTES

CHAPTER 27

Humility

"If my people, who are called by my name, will humble themselves and pray and seek my face and turn from their wicked ways, then I will hear from heaven, and I will forgive their sin and will heal their land." 2 Chronicles 7:14

Humility is not putting yourself down. True humility is having a realistic evaluation of yourself, recognizing your gifts and putting them to good use in serving God and others. It is difficult to humble ourselves when we face adversities, but our response is to stand firm and focus on God. We must turn from our prideful ways and change. Here are a few ways to practice humility. We can help others to succeed, we can learn from others and we can have the heart to serve. When we do our part and then stand back so that God can do his part, we are letting him take control. And when God does his part, amazing things happen.

Lord, I humble myself before you and recognize that I can't do anything without you. Work through all that's going on in my life to prepare me for what is ahead. In Jesus name, Amen.

NOTES

_____

CHAPTER 28

Offerings and Tithes

"Each of you should give what you have decided in your heart to give, not reluctantly or under compulsion, for God loves a cheerful giver." 2 Corinthians 9:7

There is a distinct difference between tithes and offerings. "Tithe" means a tenth or ten percent of your increase. The principle behind your tithes is that you're recognizing God as your source of supply. It's important that you give your tithe to the place that feeds you spiritually. Offerings are gifts brought to God beyond the tithes. The amount is not set. An offering is something that you decide to give to God because you love him and appreciate what he has done in your life.

One of the biggest reasons why people have a hard time being faithful in their tithes and offerings is because they don't feel like they can afford it, or they look at all of the things they need and want first. This type of thinking is basically telling God that you don't trust him to provide for all of your needs. When you begin being faithful in your tithes and offerings to God, you will receive his blessings and his favor.

Lord, make me a cheerful giver of all my tithes and offerings. Let me give with an attitude of gratitude and worship. In Jesus name, Amen.

NOTES

_____

CHAPTER 29

Freedom

"It is for freedom that Christ has set us free. Stand firm, then, and do not let yourselves be burdened again by a yoke of slavery." Galatians 5:1

You don't have to go through life feeling empty and unwanted. You don't have to be unhappy or lonely. You don't have to feel unloved. God wants you free from pain, bondage and sin. He has so much for you. He has great plans for you. He loves you very much. It's time to stop running away from him. It's time to make some changes in your life. It's time to break free from fear and shame. Do you want to experience true freedom in your life today? Accept Jesus Christ as your Lord and Savior.

Lord, I believe that Jesus died for my sins on the cross. I now repent for all of my sins. In this very moment, I receive and confess Jesus Christ as my personal Lord and Savior. May your will be done in my life. I want to experience true freedom in you. In Jesus name, Amen.

NOTES

CHAPTER 30

Fearfully and Wonderfully made

"For you created my inmost being; you knit me together in my mother's womb. I praise you because I am fearfully and wonderfully made; your works are wonderful, I know that full well." Psalm 139:13-14

You are worthy of love.
You are powerful and strong.
You are unique and brave.
You are worth more than you
could ever imagine.

You are worth more than the
number of stars in the sky.
You are worth more than the
precious stones of the earth.
He knew you before you were
in your mother's womb.
He knew the color of your eyes.
He knew the sound of your voice.
He knew the story of your tears.
He knew the music of your heartbeat.
You are his masterpiece.
He placed love inside of you and
that love will change people.
You will bring change to
this broken world.
Regardless of how you
think of yourself.

Regardless of what anyone
has told you.
No matter how many times you looked in
the mirror and wished for perfection.
He made you beautiful.

NOTES

_____

CPSIA information can be obtained at www.ICGtesting.com
Printed in the USA
BVOW04s1520160315

391881BV00001B/3/P